Teacher's note: Have children trace over the letter and colour the picture when the study of the focus letter is complete.

Channel

Trace over

Channel

Trace over

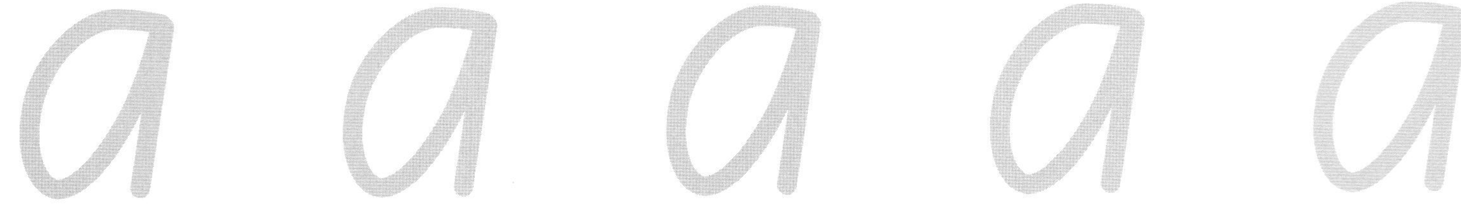

Copy

Trace over

ant ant ant

Aa

Bb

Channel

b b b b b

Trace over

b b b b b

Copy

b

Trace over

bee bee bee

Channel

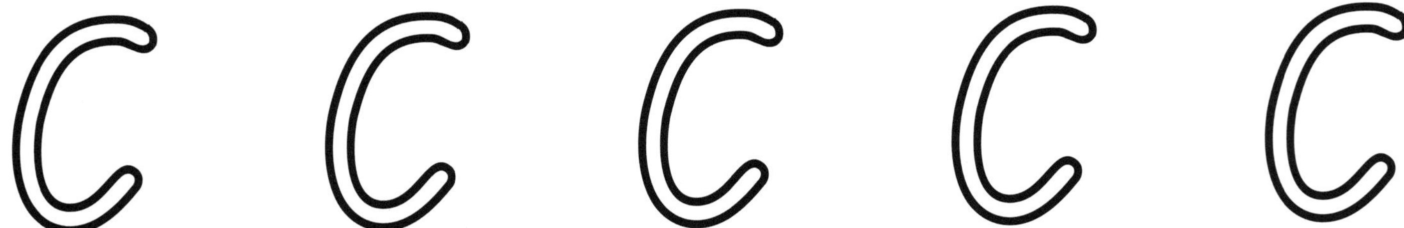

Trace over

c c c c c

Copy

c

Trace over

cake cake cake

Cc

Dd

Channel

d d d d d

Trace over

d d d d d

Copy

d

Trace over

dog dog dog

Channel

e    

Trace over

e e e e e

Copy

e

Trace over

ears ears ears

Ee

Ff

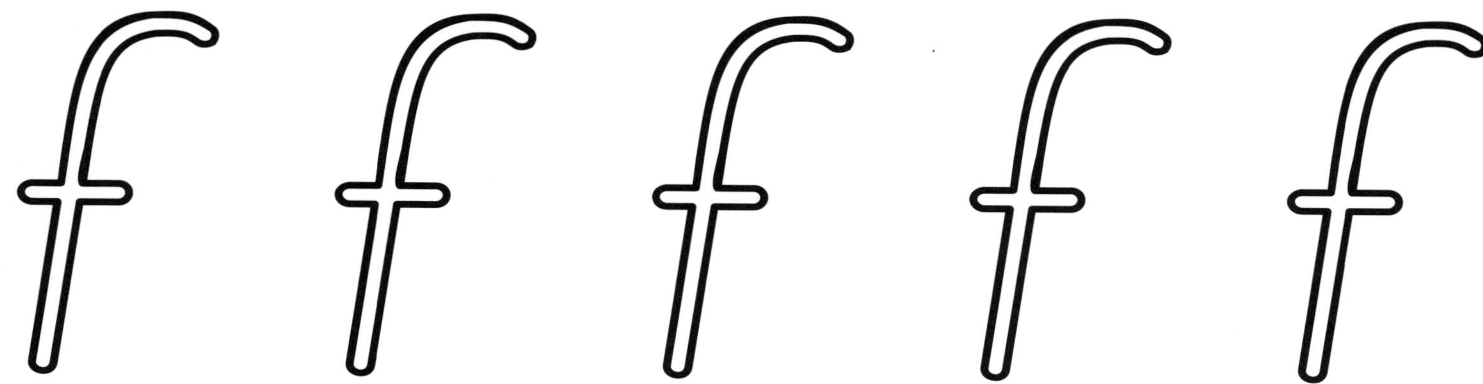

Trace over

f f f f f

Copy

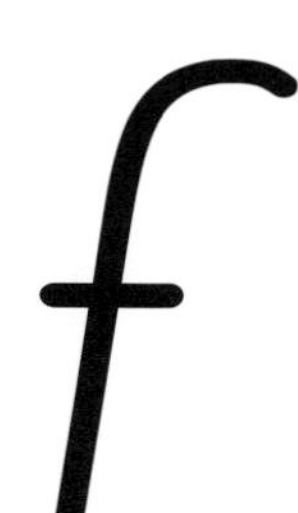

Trace over

foot foot foot

Channel

g    

Trace over

g g g g g

Copy

g

Trace over

goat goat goat

Gg

Hh

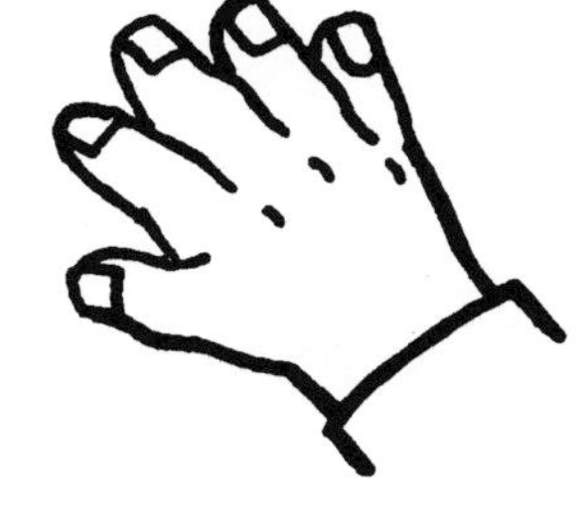

Channel

h h h h h

Trace over

h h h h h

Copy

Trace over

hand hand hand

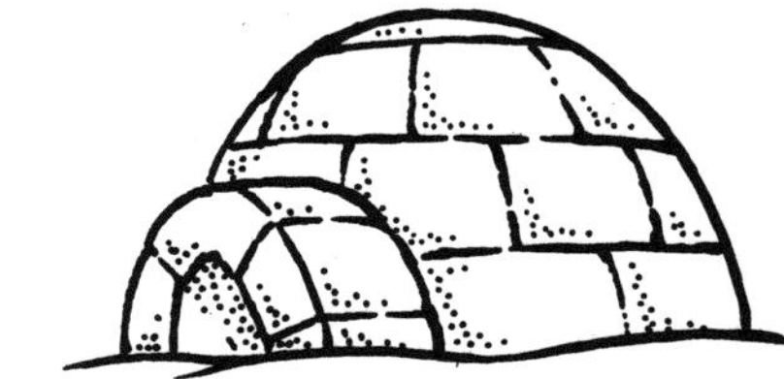

Channel

Trace over

Copy

Trace over

igloo igloo igloo

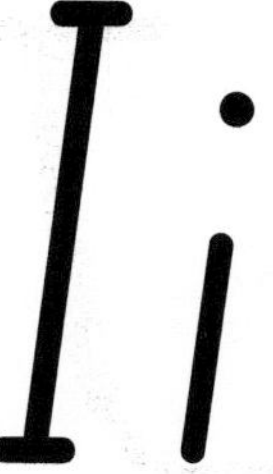

Jj

Channel

Trace over

Copy

Trace over

jigsaw jigsaw

Channel

k k k k k

Trace over

k k k k k

Copy

k

Trace over

king king king

Kk

Channel

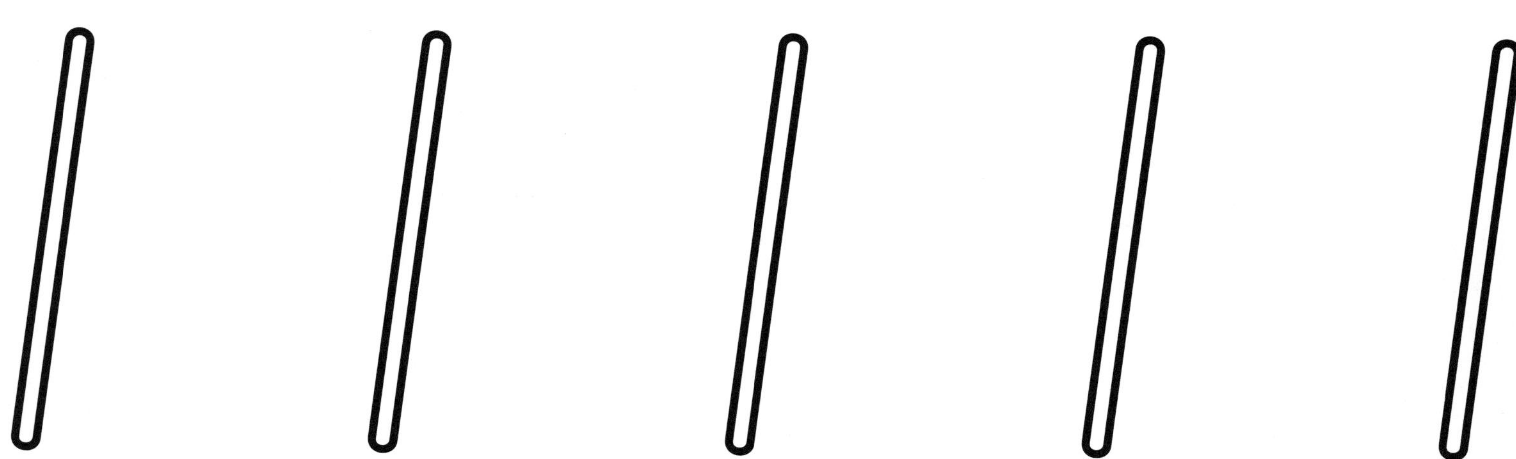

Trace over

Copy

Trace over

lips lips lips

Channel

m m m m

Trace over

Copy

Trace over

mouse mouse

Mm

Nn

Channel

n n n n n

Trace over

n n n n n

Copy

n

Trace over

nest nest nest

Channel

o 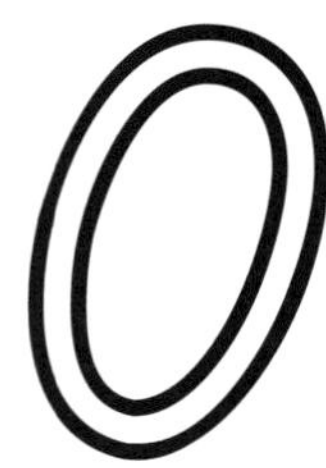 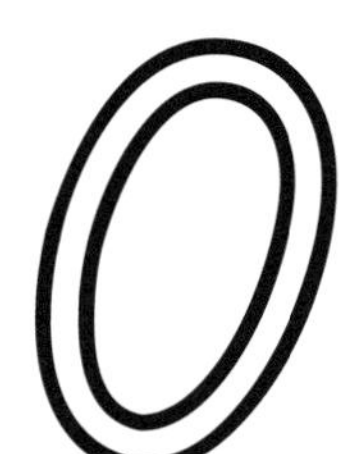 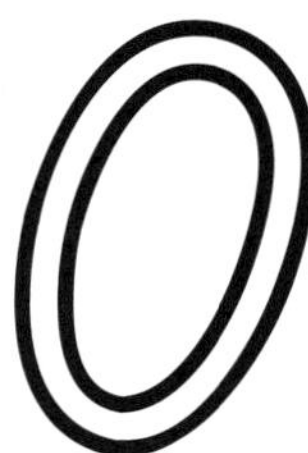 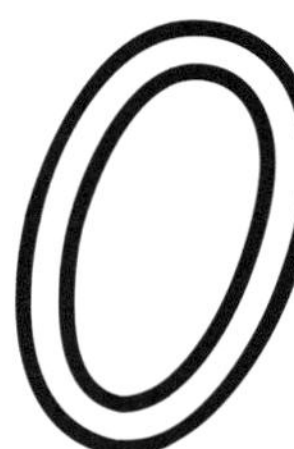

Trace over

o o o o o

Copy

o

Trace over

octopus octopus

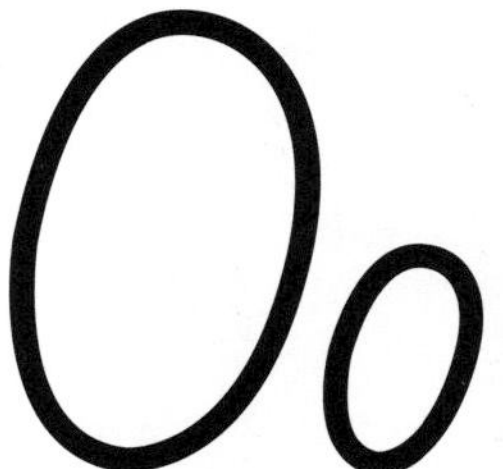

Pp

Channel

p p p p p

Trace over

p p p p p

Copy

p

Trace over

pig pig pig

Channel

q q q q q

Trace over

q q q q q

Copy

q

Trace over

queen queen

Qq

Rr

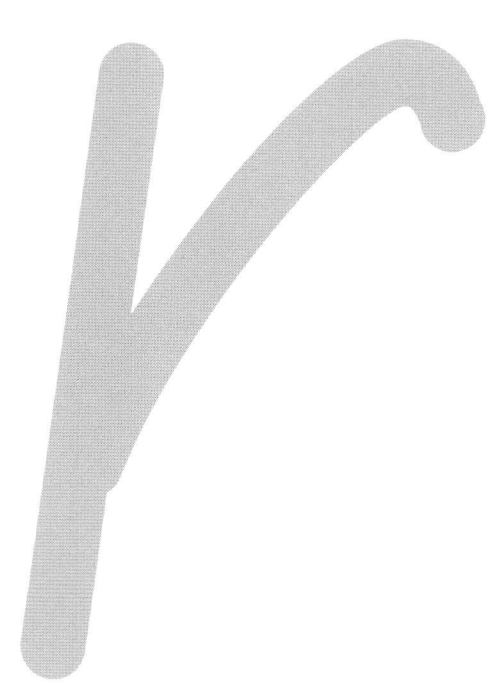

Channel

r r r r r

Trace over

r r r r r

Copy

r

Trace over

rabbit rabbit

Channel

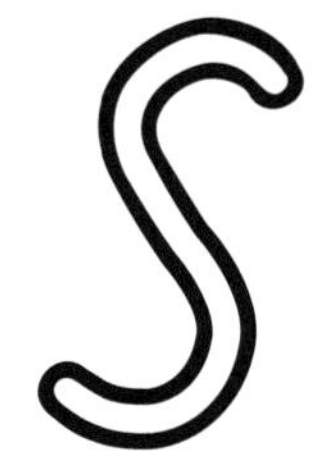    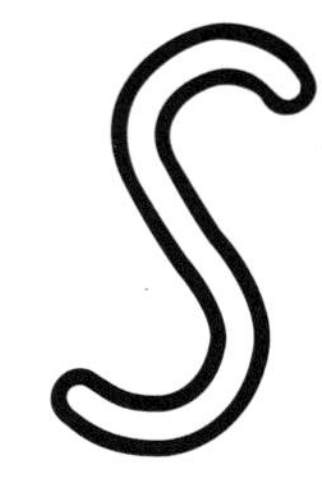

Trace over

s    

Copy

s

Trace over

snake snake

Ss

Tt

Channel

t t t t t

Trace over

Copy

Trace over

tent tent tent

Channel

u u u u u

Trace over

u u u u u

Copy

u

Trace over

umbrella umbrella

Uu

Channel

v v v v v

Trace over

v v v v v

Copy

v

Trace over

vet vet vet

Channel

w w w w

Trace over

w w w w

Copy

w

Trace over

wand wand

Ww

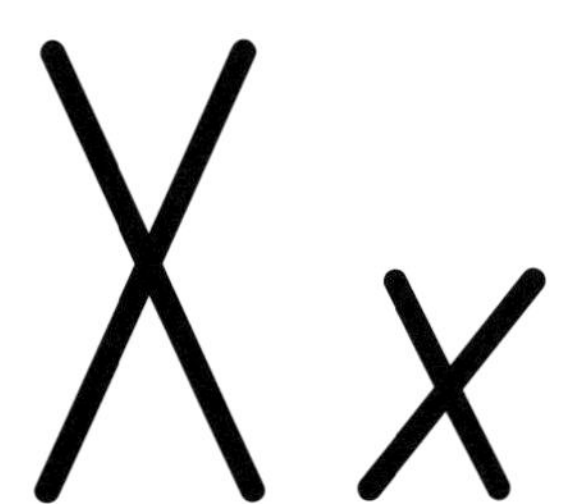

Channel

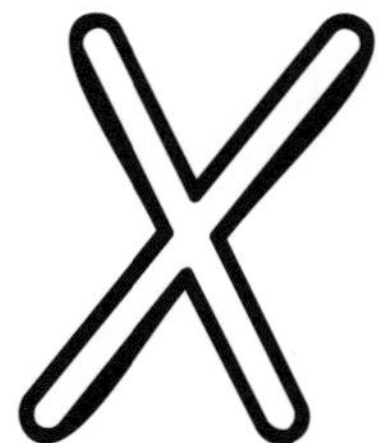    

Trace over

Copy

Trace over

y y y y y

Trace over

y y y y y

Copy

y

Trace over

yacht yacht

Yy

Zz

Channel

Z Z Z Z Z

Trace over

Z Z Z Z Z

Copy

Z

Trace over

zebra zebra

Find and trace over the letters of the alphabet. Colour the picture.